# MY LIFE AS A FOR SALE SIGN

Malcolm R. Hodson

Michael Terence Publishing

This edition published by
Michael Terence Publishing in 2020
www.mtp.agency

Copyright © 2020 Malcolm R. Hodson

Malcolm R. Hodson has asserted his right to be identified as the
author of this work in accordance with the
Copyright, Designs and Patents Act 1988

ISBN 9781913289836

No part of this publication may be reproduced, stored in a retrieval
system, or transmitted, in any form or by any means, electronic,
mechanical, photocopying, recording or otherwise, without the prior
permission of the publishers

Cover images
Copyright © Alexcoolok, Feverpitched

Cover design
Copyright © 2019 Michael Terence Publishing

To all the everyday heroes

who keep us all safe and well…

# MY LIFE AS A FOR SALE SIGN

Malcolm R. Hodson

## Contents

1: ME!.................................................................. 1

2: MY NEW OWNERS ............................................. 4

3: ALL CHANGE .................................................... 10

4: THIS MUST BE A MISTAKE ........................... 15

5: THANK GOODNESS; ANYONE FOR AN ICE CREAM?................................................................. 19

6: THE SHOP ......................................................... 26

7: WOW! IS THIS REAL? ...................................... 33

8: THAT CAN'T BE TRUE! CAN IT? ................. 36

9: BLESS YOU! ...................................................... 40

## 1: ME!

Seeing as we are going to get acquainted you may call me Sign. At this stage, I'm still in a great big factory that makes lots of different kinds of wooden signs. The factory is based up North somewhere, unless, of course, you live on the Shetland Isles or even most of Scotland come to that. Then it would be down South.

Initially, I was in a large forest in Sweden where I grew up with all my family and mates. There were thousands of us quite happily growing, minding our own business, doing our bit for the ecosystem and wildlife.

One day out of the blue the biggest saw you've ever seen in your life came along and cut us down. They did at least promise that they would plant new ones. Sustainability seems to be the new buzz word going around. (See the FSE web site for more details).

We were cut into large planks of timber, before being transported via big lorries to the docks where we then got exported to the UK.

Before you even ask, yes, the journey by sea was very unpleasant. Seriously that salt water gets everywhere. Then there's the unloading at the other end.

Upon arrival at the giant factory, we are stacked and stored before the big day comes. Yes, I along with many others are put through various machines, they cut, saw plane and sort, all before moving down the line to the next department. It's quite a quick painless procedure all though it can get very noisy at times.

Anyway, let's fast forward a little as I've just had my new exterior grade plywood attached. At last, I feel whole again as if one has a purpose. Being one of the better signs (Grade A, I'll have you know) Of course I still have several layers of paint to be applied, one would imagine by hand. Bright sunshine yellow with a Sorrento red border and LOOK-OUTS estate agents stencilled on in royal blue. A phone number and get this, a web address. With my brilliant white post, one must say, one looks really very smart. Some of my inferior cousins are made from plastic as it is claimed they can be recycled and are better for the environment. I can't help feeling it's a matter of choice; (well it's about the quality really).

Once in the dispatch area, hundreds of signs are waiting to be transported to our new owners all over the UK. I myself, are going further down south to Inter-County-Sign-Services-limited plc.

Depending on which team is loading makes a massive difference as to how well you are handled; luckily, I've been loaded by Shirana. She appears to take great care in loading us up being very careful to ensure our bright new shiny paintwork doesn't get chipped.

Slam! Goes the lorry door as darkness now falls all around us. (It's a good job I don't get travel sick).

## 2: MY NEW OWNERS

The doors open and beautiful bright sunlight comes flooding in prior to being unloaded. There's just a small group of us here being dropped off here at the Boding Hampton depot. Our new owners seem very pleased to see us, as even the store manager popped out to inspect us. Along with his secretary who commented on how smart my paintwork looked (well ours).

"Most of these will be out by tomorrow." Announced Yandip, to the truck driver, who after a quick cup of tea drove off to his next destination.

Once all stacked up nice and neat in our specially made racks, looking around I could see hundreds of other types of signs. Some I have to say looking very worse for wear and dare I even use the term… uncared for. (Really! it should be a criminal offence).

The day started early, about seven- thirty with the sun shining and listening carefully, one could hear the odd bird singing. I had a good happy feeling that things were going to be OK. Within a few minutes the nice young man Yandip, backed his big white van up to the racks, where my colleagues and I had slept over-night. After checking his clipboard at least twice, I was chosen along with a few others to be put in the van. The radio played classical music and I have to admit, it made for a very nice journey. Not too loud either, unlike some of the cars we encountered at traffic lights. Yes!... at the moment Yandip is coming across as a very pleasant, polite, courteous driver. We had to pull over at one point for Yandip to answer the phone, it was his wife I assume asking him to get some milk on the way home. I say wife because whoever it was, he told them he loved them lots and would see them tonight.

Finally, it was my turn to get unloaded (not bad hey, being the fourth of the van). With great care, being placed perfectly straight and upright, I'd been put to work outside a very nice detached property, on a rather nice street. Trees and mature gardens with a large grass area to the front and rear, along with a garage and driveway. First impressions are that I can't see me being here for long at all. What with the double glazing a newly fitted kitchen, even the neighbours house's all seem very well cared for.

Two of the neighbours came out, (you know the nosey one's) I can only assume they wanted my details, you know, name and phone number etc. One of them seemed quite put out by the fact they had not been informed, that the house was even going on the market, whereas Mrs Button at number twenty-two had.

After only a few minutes the conversation turned to Miss Phillip's daughter going off to university, before the other one boasted that their son was a hair-dresser and has cut several famous footballer's hair. When pressed on the matter, it turns out its no one we'd heard of. Needless to say, a bragging match took place for the next ten minutes.

Only four days had passed before two view-ees and the estate agent were here to have a look around. Thankfully the weather has been extremely kind to us so far, hot sunny days have blessed us all. I have to admit I'm not looking forward to the cold, wet weather later in the year, as for the snow it makes me shudder just thinking about it.

Morning five dawned only to be rudely awakened by the dustbin men, who did no less than push a wheelie bin into my tall white support; thankfully I received no marks or scuffs. On reflection it could have been a lot worse though, as only a few moments earlier a great big dog came up and relieved itself, up the wheelie bin. Why it couldn't use the tree like most dogs do, I don't know.

People walk by, some taking my number, one or two even take photos of me. (Now you might think it's my number their after, but deep down I know it's just me they want a photo of).

The gossip you hear is unbelievable, some funny, some very serious and don't for one moment think it's just the ladies who like to natter. A lot of the old guys go on for ages, discussing all manner of topics from ingrowing toenails to their best mate's hip replacement. But by far the most common subject is how short the skirts were on the dancing program the other night and that they weren't allowed to wear skirts that short in their day.

A couple more days have now passed and of course, it had to happen. Yes, I'm talking rain; rain by the bucketful. I suppose the one good thing to take from it, is not to have to see the dogs relieve themselves up the tree in front of me or sniff around the bottom of my pole. Still, I do look nice and gleaming again now that at last it's stopped. With the sun coming back out again, memories returned with it. I recall my homeland back in the deep lush forest, happily growing away with my other sibling. (Well full-size trees actually).

I'd lived there for many years as I was moved from a nursery being just a wee sapling. Once planted, we had virtually no human contact as we were commercially grown on a large forest plantation which was out of bounds to the public. My cousins and I did have some friends though, Doraphe the deer with her very large family, lots of different birds. One or two of the older trees told stories of wild boar and big cats roaming around, but I think they were just pulling our roots (leg). Oh, there was my great friend Cyril the Squirrel who took great pleasure in running up and down me. I made up a daft rhyme about him.

## *CYRIL, THE SQUIRREL*

If I was a squirrel living in a tree,
I'd climb up to the top to see what I could see.

On the way back down I'd spiral round and round,
To the very bottom where I'd finally reach the ground.

I'd look all around and everywhere as well,
Just to find a bite to eat; a nut would be swell.

My homes up high and hidden very much out of the way,
All warm and cosy as I hate the rain, what more can I say.

With the sun back out, now it's time for me to play and jump,
As long as I go carefully, I shouldn't get a bump.

# SOLD

My that was quick; Yandip is here already putting a sold sign over me.

At this rate I'll be moving again soon. (Have I ever told you, I love travelling).

## 3: ALL CHANGE

The next property I was attached to, (well its garden gate) was next door but two from the towns Fire Station.

It's a quaint semi-detached house that I believe used to be an old Police house. Yes, I know it seems strange but at one time the police used to own a lot of properties. Having three bedrooms, a big kitchen and generous sized lounge, very well-kept gardens to the front and rear. Along with the garage and driveway, it appears to be a lovely little house.

Most of the time being on the outskirts of the town it was very quiet and peaceful. Until that is, Tuesday night. Yes, you've guessed it, Tuesday night is drill night. Honestly, the Fire Station yard became so busy, what with the firefighters' cars, plus bringing the fire engine round there wasn't much room by the time they'd finished. Cutting up cars, climbing up ladders and often spraying water everywhere, for a few hours it was all very exciting.

Days would go by without any activity what-so-ever and other weeks they could be out two or three times a day. In the short few weeks (which as I recall was only about six) I had the pleasure of advertising and selling the house, only one person came to view me. They, in turn, put an offer in straight away. I believe she was a firefighter. So, no surprise there then.

A visiting school party from the local primary school arrived mid-morning for a talk on fire safety. Station Officer Blaze along with Firefighter Hotter, were tasked with the talk and slide show followed by a question and answer session.

One question, which was asked by a young girl was…

"Do you still rescue animals?"

"Over to you Firefighter Hotter," Came the command from S.O Blaze with a very raised eyebrow and dry smile.

"Oh yes, one day we had to rescue a cat stuck up a tree, which had been chased by next doors dog. Now that wasn't the initial call out. The first calls received were for something totally different. You see it wasn't really his fault, as the dog had jumped over the fence due to being frightened by a loud bang going off, which was caused by an explosion in the paint shop of the car repair place, on the industrial estate on the other side of town.

It turns out a new trainee made the mistake of putting an additional gas heater in one of the paint spray booths, to help keep the temperature up. Only to then knock over a very large can of thinners, this, in turn, caused a small fire. Unfortunately, the thinners ran across the floor to where additional drums of thinners were being stored. He ran to get help and raise the alarm only to find his workmates had gone on their tea break. By the time they got back downstairs to help a serious fire had now taken hold.

Needless to say, within minutes the whole factory along with the next two units had to be evacuated. Multiple loud explosions could be heard all across town. Five pumps later, a hydraulic platform plus command unit, with much hard work the blaze was bought under control. Thankfully no one was hurt. On the way back to the station, Appliance 325 (that's ours) was flagged down by Mrs Brockley at number sixteen, to ask if they could help get her kitty - Pereleen down from up a tree, outside the front of her house."


Sometimes they just went out for a drive to go and check on certain things and would return fairly soon after leaving. (Routine checks and all that sort of thing). Once they turned left out of the station, but five minutes later came flying back with all lights flashing and siren screaming, straight past the station towards the town. It was the lady firefighter driving and very, very fast too.

I'm pretty sure she must be an ex formula one driver never mind a fire engine driver.

If they'd been gone a long time the lovely old man from down the road would come to the station to keep an eye on things, plus put all their shoes nice and neat by the lockers. One couldn't help but worry, hoping everything was OK and that all would work out well, for everyone involved. Only the other day whilst anxiously waiting for them to return I made up a verse.

## *QUICK, QUICK, EMERGENCY*

The BIG RED FIRE ENGINE makes such a noise,
It has to get there quickly, it doesn't have a choice.

Turning right out the station heading straight for the town,
Rushing down the road before turning left; by the rose and crown.

It has to go that way; it's a one-way street,
Chances are, the crew will wave to those sat on the seat.

If it's nothing major, they'll be back fairly soon,
But when they're gone a long time, you'd think they've gone to the moon.

Yes! I'm sure it's not far and they know exactly where,
As long as when they get there, they take every care.

Once more my SOLD sign was attached to me. One thing I did think was a little strange was it wasn't Yandip come to pick me up a few weeks later. Thankfully the journey back to the yard was reasonably quick and uneventful, just me and a few other signs. However, one poor sign was telling me of his last experience and that he wished never to return to that area again.

That will never happen to me!... Obviously being assigned to one of the more select estate agents, I kept thinking to myself.

## 4: THIS MUST BE A MISTAKE

WRONG…WRONG … WRONG, how could you be so wrong? Well, I'll tell you how!

It was a damp cold morning when I got pulled out of my storage rack and thrown, yes thrown into the back of Dave's van. This is not a good start to the day and where the devil is Yandip anyway. I clearly recall thinking to myself. What with music blasting out, slamming on the brakes, driving down the road like Herbert- van- wrecker, I thought at this rate I'll be glad to get to my new assignment. After holding on really tight, yes! this is definitely the second thought now entering my mind and being pushed right to the front, almost as quick as this van's being driven.

Not that Dave was any gentler putting me up, luckily nowadays we have new super long tie wraps (you know, the ones long enough to go round your house, well not quite!) No more nasty holes being drilled into you, not mention the screws.

I should have known my luck had to change sometime. It turns out I've been put up outside a house, or at least been tie-wrapped to a rusty metal gate post. No gate; just a rusty post. I'm in the middle of a very busy cut through road in one of those less desirable areas of town.

A two bedroom flat on the upper floor, as if things couldn't get much worse, there were other For Sale signs up. Yes! I know at least six other For Sale signs and dare I even say it, a *To Let* sign.

Now how can I possibly be the centre of attention when one has to compete under such circumstances? Within five minutes I had a dog relieve itself right next to me. And there was litter scattered down the street. Why humans have to go around dropping litter is beyond me. (It's their rubbish; they should take it home to dispose of).

Night time came and went, which was equally as interesting. Needless to say, it was incredibly busy right up to after midnight and morning rush hour seems to start at about six o'clock.

One thing I noticed whilst watching this ever-busy world of ours go by; was an elderly gentleman took very ill in the street one early morning. Falling to the ground; one hand on his chest the other trying to grab the fence for support. Within seconds people were coming out to help him, three then four rushed over to help, even a car and its driver stopped to help, declaring he was a nurse. Moments later sirens blaring a Police car came roaring down the street, two officers walked briskly across to see what assistance they could give. One was instantly on his radio; whilst his colleague thanked the local people who called for help, along with their kindness, showing such care and compassion. It's great to know that normally when somebody desperately needs help calls are answered with great kindness.

Only four or five minutes later an ambulance arrived, and the female paramedic immediately and professionally took charge of the old man's care, bringing a sense of relief to the situation.

Listening intently, I could hear locals talking amongst themselves and to the police, as to who the elderly gentleman was and where he lived. It turns out he's a lovely old man who lives down the next road on his own, since his wife died last year. Being very lonely, he now loves to stop and chat with people and would do anything to help you.

After a short time, the patient was placed carefully and safely into the back of the ambulance. The female paramedic told her colleague a young black paramedic "We need to get cracking Desmond"

Now I don't know whether this was code or something but without further ado, Desmond jumped in the cab after ensuring all the doors were securely shut and had a quick word to the police officer. The ambulance than shot off down the road, sirens wailing for all to hear, as the blue lights danced off the house windows, their mesmerising reflections illuminated the whole street. Cars lorries and even buses feverishly scurried out of Desmond's way.

I'm in no doubt what so ever that when he gets to the hospital all possible care will be given to him by the wonderful doctors and nurses, who work tirelessly to make us humans better again. (Well not me of course, I'm a piece of wood).

# 5: THANK GOODNESS; ANYONE FOR AN ICE CREAM?

At about ten thirty to my total surprise, an inter-county signs van pulled up outside number seven, whereupon two gentlemen got out and started to look up and down the street at house numbers. Within a matter of moments, my cable ties were cut and once more I was placed in the van. While the other man put a sign up in my place. Who these chaps are I haven't a clue. One did look rather smart though, which made me wonder if he was a boss or manager. The trip back to the yard seemed to take forever, stopping on route to collect other signs, it was getting on for mid-afternoon by the time I'd been unloaded and stored away in the racks. Thankfully these two were a bit more gentle.

Busy earwigging (I mean overhearing) it became apparent that as I guessed, there'd been an almighty mistake and I shouldn't have been taken to that place at all.

At about five thirty, I can't tell you how relieved I was to see Yandip's van pull into the yard. It was quite obvious that he'd come for me, as I reassured myself with a smug warm feeling now running all the way through me.

But hold on a minute, other signs are being put in the van first. First one, then another, even one of those new internet sign thingy jobs. This cannot be happening, not after the ordeal I've just been through.

Lastly, but by NO WAY last I was placed securely into the nice special storage racks in Yandip's van. We were then parked up in the yard overnight.

The journey although quite long seemed uneventful, apart from the horrible weather. Unfortunately, it was still raining and fairly windy, not to mention as grey as slate when we arrived at my new assignment. Considering it was only late morning, you'd think it was the middle of the night.

Being barely able to work out my new property I'm selling, the one thing one could not fail to notice is the noise (or should I say racket from the seagulls) and the smell of seaweed, fish and chips plus the rock, you know sticks of rock.

Thankfully Friday morning dawned clear and bright, so with the sun shining, dry patches emerging, puddles disappearing one couldn't help but have one's spirits lifted. Looking out to sea with a lighthouse on the horizon, it got me thinking, 'If that place ever comes for sale, who's going to put the sign out there?'

Days came and went as did the tourist, even the circus rolled into town for a week. So many different noises and smells dominated the air that week. Candy floss, toffee apples and of course diesel fumes from the generators. Fish and chips certainly took second place that week. (Apparently, other food outlets are available).

As darkness fell one cold damp autumn evening, the clouds suddenly changed direction and the wind began to pick up, coming directly off the sea. I clearly recall thinking to myself; I don't like what's happening, this is not good. Within a very short time, a full force hurricane had developed. I was unable to stop shuddering from the battering of the wind. I decided to prepare for the worse, believing things aren't supposed to stop up in this.

5 a.m. saw the sun begin to rise; as though it too had been taking shelter for the night. Miraculously I was still standing tall, upright and completely intact. Some of the poor trees and bushes took a right pounding though, a few looked very much worse for wear. Litter was strewn across the road, where a number of plastic litter bins decided to take flight in the early hours. Council workers being the good Samaritans they are swept and tidied

feverishly like an ant colony on a time schedule, till once more all looked well. (As if to say; what storm?)

Three or four young couples, a young family along with several elderly couples came to view this delightful three-bedroom house, with its beautiful big bay windows. Full of charm and character, surely somebody must buy it soon. It's a lot of money though, as are all properties that are by the seaside or even near the coast come to that. I suppose a lot of it is because many people would like to retire to the coast.

On at least three or four occasions the lifeboat station sprang into life. Whenever that siren goes off, things become a whirlwind of activity. (Perhaps whirlwind is not quite the correct term). Anyway, I believe they have two lifeboats here, one being a big all-weather Aran class. The other being an Atlantic 21, which is more for inshore quick response duties. Having said that both are very fast, even the tractors that help launch them into the water doesn't hang about. Within minutes these brave souls are launched and off. They work alongside the rescue helicopter and the coastguard, who are also mainly volunteers. At the end of the day, it's all about helping each other. May I add, it's this fantastic teamwork, trust in your fellow colleagues and knowing that everyone involved is trying their utmost to get a successful outcome, that normally gets a successful outcome.

With the onset of winter upon us, unfortunately as already experienced bad weather was never far away. I'm fairly sure that on Tuesday it rained all day, most of Wednesday morning too, as I recall. What with the rain, sea mist and biting winds it can make the whole place seem rather bleak at times. Then, of course, the sea also likes to make its presence known, you can hear the waves crashing against the giant wooden breakwaters that stand so proud doing their duty the best they can. Talk about a battering the noise produced as endless ferocious waves go pounding into the concrete promenade is enough to make you shudder.

It was late Thursday evening; after what has to be said was a cold, very grey, rainy and unpleasant day. It really was turning into a shocking night. Gale force winds pouring with rain and waves half as big as this house. The Claxton went off followed by the siren at the lifeboat station. As always, the crew are there in force within minutes. The big Aran class was launched; it really is magnificent to see the skill, teamwork and professionalism to get this beautiful looking boat launched. One can't help but worry though, it got me thinking.

*When the bleeper goes off they all come running.*

*At the lifeboat station things happen really quickly.*

Winston, Sam, Johnathon and even Aunt Beryl.
They're on their way out to help those in great peril.

In the baking hot sun, mountainous seas or even lashing with rain,
They still always go out to help all those, who may well, be in pain.

Once everyone is safe and back on dry land,
Oh, to feel that warm yellow stuff, I believe it's called sand.

No wind, snow or fog, will ever stop these brave selfless folk
Before finishing their ordeal they'll still have time for a joke

Once home nice and safe, getting warm drinking a hot cup of tea,
You don't need to remind these heroes of the dangers of the sea.

I'll be sorry to leave this place, to say that it grows on you would not at all be an exaggeration. But you know how it is, a new month and a new property to sell. Oh yes, of course, I forgot to tell you! That lovely old couple bought the house, so no doubt that the grandkids will be visiting in the holidays.

One thing I won't miss; is that freezing cold wind.

## 6: The shop

Although officially its winter the weather has been very kind to me, December and there are still a few leaves on the trees. Thankfully the winds around here are much calmer than in my last location. A carpet of multi-coloured leaves covered parts of the pavement though, where a small gentle whirlwind had placed them to rest. The cheery old council worker once more comes along with his worn-out looking brush and wheeled cart. (Which to be honest is more like the Tardis, with the amount of stuff he puts in it). Ten minutes later it's as bad again, although I don't mind to me it just adds colour to the place.

Anyway, about this shop, well no it's not actually a shop but an apartment above it. When I say apartment; I mean apartment. Three bedrooms, two living rooms plus a very large newly refurbished kitchen. It has got its own entrances at the rear of the shop complete with parking spaces for three cars specially reserved for its owners. I'm led to believe that up until about seven years ago it was the first floor of what was once a very grand department store. Nowadays the shops only a quarter of the size it used to be and that's just one floor, so storage is no longer an issue. No doubt the previous owners sold the upper floors off, oh yes there's another one above this one. With the ground floor now being rented out, this has had several tenants over the years.

The floors being listed;

Basement

Ground floor

First floor

Second floor, and with a large lift to access each floor.

Now there's a term you don't hear very much nowadays, (no, not shop… Basement).

As I've said, the floor area of this place is massive, with the master bedroom measuring twenty feet by thirty feet. Bearing in mind there's another two, along with a lounge that's over thirty feet long; a huge kitchen, you could have a game of cricket in it. All this and stunning views out the enormous windows, to watch a busy city go by, right below you. In the few short weeks I've been here, some of the stories one's heard are frequently repeated by the older generation stopping for a chat, reminiscing about the good old days. Memories are exchanged of how the store would hold just one big sale in January, that's right just one, not like these days when it seems every other week there's a sale on. I think soon they'll have to have a sale to sell and get rid of all the SALE signs. Super Sale, Mega Sale, Super Mega Sale, you name it Sale. I tell you there must be thousands of them.

One incredibly moving story I did hear of (no pun intended!)

There is a very interesting plaque on the outside wall, at the front of the shop in the shape of an old-fashioned helmet with two names on it. It gets cleaned every other week by an elderly gentleman who comes along. He stops, stares at the sign for a few moments before taking out a cloth from his coat pocket and gives the sign a wipe as if polishing it. Sometimes he brings his grandson along. The story behind this is one of immense bravery…

It turns out that during the Second World War, two auxiliary firemen were dealing with a blaze across the road, with their colleagues, when another stray bomb hit this building.

Screams and shouts for help could be heard even above all the other commotion going on. Without any regard for their own safety; the two firemen entered the shop, hoping to gain access to the first floor, where they believed the cries were coming from.

Locating the family, two adults and a young child who had taken refuge in the shop, as the young child had become terrified by all the noise and chaos from the first bomb exploding. The poor young family had only gone for an afternoon walk; nobody expected anything like this to happen.

Thankfully mum and child were not too badly injured but very much in shock, where-as poor old dad was in quite a bad way after taking the full force of the falling brickwork whilst protecting his wife and child.

Charlie managed to crawl on his tummy across the debris and missing floorboards, to where the three were huddled in a corner clinging to each other, unable to move, shaking and terrified with fear.
Syd the other fireman meanwhile got to the window, by moving several pieces of furniture which now looked more like firewood. After much shouting and waving he got the attention of the fireman working the turntable ladder. Within minutes the top of the ladder was resting on the window ledge. Mum and toddler were rescued first, assisted by another fireman down the ladder. Charlie somehow managed to get dad to where Syd stood by the window, by almost pushing him across the floor. With much screaming in pain, trembling with fear Syd finally got dad with the help of the other fireman on the ladder, only to then hear an almighty crash. Turning

around instantly; he found Charlie hanging by his fingertips onto one of the floor joists, amongst a cloud of dust. As Syd lunged to grab hold of Charlie, the whole floor gave way. Both firemen fell two floors onto a pile of rubbish and debris below them. The sound of a collapsing wall could be heard far too easily for all, as the biggest part of one of the main supporting walls disappeared into a pile of rubbish and dust.

Time froze, as no more noise could be heard, be that by a human, or building. Just cold desperate, empty silence fell upon the street; only the faint distant ringing of the ambulance bell whizzing dad off to hospital could be heard.

It was the next morning before the bodies of Charlie and Syd were found.

---

Young girls would take up jobs after leaving school, probably even work with a family member, mum aunt or even an older sister. Between them, many years' service would be put in. Forty years plus, service was not unheard of. The store becoming so much more than just a job, indeed for some this was their only job, the only job they knew. Work, pleasure, even love was found by some, meeting a storeroom man or perhaps a regular customer, a delivery driver, who knows. Stories going around; talk of a social club, bingo and games nights, days out to the seaside and of course Christmas parties.

All this got me thinking;


This wonderful old store always opened at nine on the dot,
With it being such a big store it employed quite a lot.

Selling furniture, all sizes of beds and even fancy stools,
With an area in the basement; selling quality hand tools.

A great selection of haberdashery, Linen, cotton and yarns of wool,
All the helpful staff who worked here, were really wonderful.


As you can see from the list they sold almost everything,
Including a music department, so you could learn how to sing.

The store even played music, so you might hear your favourite song,
But sadly like all so many things, unfortunately it's now gone.

Talking of Christmas, I can't believe this place has sold so quick at this time of year. Put up in December, taken down in January, goodness me it's a busy life.

## 7: WOW! IS THIS REAL?

Having been tucked away all snug and bug for the rest of the winter (well till the end of March anyway). It would appear that we're going out for a drive in the country, thankfully my old pall Yandip is still my chauffeur. Don't ask me how we got here, travelling down motorways, up two very busy A roads, then through what appeared to be a bustling little market town, before going out even further into the very rural countryside, just passed the quaintest little village you've ever seen.

Getting out of the van and looking around, I could hardly believe my new location. I'm outside a country mansion; with get this, its own driveway. Ornate metal railings that spread either side the main gateway for at least several hundred yards, which are choc-a-bloc full of rhododendrons, before turning into a small copse as the railings finish.

After being here four or five days, I was still in awe of my new location, the peace and tranquillity fresh air and of course silence. Mind you; there were noises; animal noises the wildlife around here is amazing. Being a big respecter of the environment and lover of nature (it must be in my genes) I'm quite happy for animals of all sorts and sizes to come up to me and have a good sniff.

Yes, I know marking of the territory is not quite so pleasant but, hay-ho!

Just a few types of animals that I encounter every day would be badgers, muntjac, deer, rabbits and hares plus the occasional foxes. Horse riders and cyclists come by daily, sometimes chatting to each other. The foxes tended to come out at night much more, probably believing it would be safer for them.

Don't you think all animals should be respected and after all, it's their planet too? They have just as much right to be here as we humans do. (Yer! granted they don't pay taxes) but even so! We've all got to live somewhere, it is called planet Earth, not planet human! Looking after the environment is everybody's responsibility.

Anyway; enough ranting for the moment. Being near to a river (well actually it's a stream across the road) one would often see ducks and swans along with many other birds even the odd heron would come and perch nearby, eagerly waiting for his dinner to swim by.

Standing here looking across the quiet little lane, beyond the fields which give off the impression of continuing on forever, I couldn't help but find myself allowing to be transported back to my motherland. The sun shone so brightly reflecting back from the stream, as if squinting like some giant mirror. With the sun beating down, it illuminated the fields up on the hill, you could almost smell and feel the warmth and richness oozing out the crops busily growing away. As for the woodlands at the rear and further down the lane, one could only dream of the wildlife, plants and trees happily growing in harmony with each other.

(Oh, how I miss my youth).

Big fancy posh cars (and their owners of course) came to look at this beautiful house, with its six bedrooms, two reception rooms, library and even a stable block. Apparently, would you believe, it is known to have in all seven toilets, or at one time called W.C for water chambers. I'm not entirely sure how much land it's got, but I'm glad I don't have to cut the grass. It must be several acres. As for the poor window cleaner, I hope he's got a big bucket. Apparently, a pop star is coming to view with their agent later today, so I heard the estate agent say, who was telling the current owners as they stood waving goodbye to some rich MP who had just popped in to have a look around.

## 8: THAT CAN'T BE TRUE! CAN IT?

Some of the stories I get to hear about from passers-by as they stop to have a chat by the gates, regarding the history and characters of this beautiful old manor house.

One such story goes…

That many years ago a rather eccentric couple lived here, no children, just the two of them. Plus of course a maid, servant and the butler, who doubled up as a chauffeur (times must have been so hard). Although they were married for some reason the pair were known by their individual names, thus being Lord Rupetus Hahra-Wego Smith and Lady Tinkerbell Topitup. One can only speculate as to how true that these names actually are. However, it was well known by all that her ladyship was rather keen on a rather fruity homemade gin. I can't say as it appeals to me, just ringing a bell and have a maid come top up my drink, due to not being able to open the new bottle, certainly at or before two in the afternoon.

Rumour has it, that's why the first chauffeur left. He was getting too old to keep having to carry her Ladyship back to the Rolls. In those days one didn't drive one's own Rolls you know. No, I'm not getting it mixed up; I don't mean the maid bringing in some bread rolls.

Lord Hahra-Wego was also very keen and it has to be said, good horse jumper. (I assume that means over fences whilst on the horse). Winning several medals and trophy's both locally and nationally, collecting reasonable prize money along the way. No doubt used to top up Lady Topitup's homemade gin reserves.

Another story I heard of; concerned a young servant boy that worked for his Lord and Ladyship only in the late forties, so quite recent when you think how old the great house is. The young boy's name was Peter, but to save time they (they being his Lord and Ladyship) decided to call all the staff by the first letter of their name. (I say all; apparently, they only had two staff anyway).

Now Peter was working one day when Great Aunt Mildred and her young, second twice-removed cousins friend came for afternoon tea. Which eventually became quite a regular thing. Now it just so happens; Rebecca, the cousins' friend, was only twenty-two, very beautiful and a bit of a tomboy at heart, as opposed to Great Aunt Mildred who looked about two hundred and ten and acted even older. She could hardly walk, had terrible eyesight and was as deaf as a post. Rebecca (the young lady) also called Bobie for short, used to assist Great Aunt Mildred in her wheelchair and with other personal tasks. Like for instance, washing, feeding and driving Great Aunt Mildred around.

Well the inevitable happened and young Peter fell head over heels madly in love with Rebecca and likewise, it has to be said, Rebecca with Peter.

Unfortunately, poor old Great Aunt Mildred became rather ill and so was unable to visit Upper-down Manor (why they just couldn't call it middle; I don't know).

This meant that Rebecca no longer had use of the car, so now had to catch the train to Winbourn Charmer a quaint little village about a mile down the road. One bright sunny afternoon Lady Pamalena Thacwkit, whilst speaking to her husband Sir Angus Ian Dipitin (known to his chums as SAID), asked: "where P was, as I need the car bringing round."

"Oh! P's gone for Bobie at the WC train station. One must say it's becoming a bit of a regular thing lately." Replied SAID.

---

Well, what with all the stories and gossip, the time has flown by. As I thought; but would you believe it, the pop star made a cash offer which has been accepted. Things seemed to move at a rather quick pace and before you knew it the removal vans were arriving.

Standing around looking at anything and everything, taking it all in, I began to wonder what fate lies ahead. Thankfully my trusty old friend Yandip has come to collect me.

## 9: BLESS YOU!

No need to go back to the depot, just a couple of stops, minor detours to erect two other signs. I'd only just began to get myself comfy in my rack in my favourite person's van when we pulled up outside the village sign.

I heard Yandip ask not so much for directions, more to confirm, what I assume is to be my new location. Biding the two old ladies a good day we drove just a few hundred yards before turning left down a little dead-end road.

I'm fairly sure we're not far from our beautiful old manor house (Upperdown Manor). A lovely, peaceful, sleepy, quaint village, probably only about ten miles away. My new location is Wendysbut chapel. Yes, you heard it right! A Chapel. Now being sold as a private dwelling, you could call it a project.

The chapel did, unfortunately, look tired as if neglect had been allowed to take hold. Dating back to nearly two hundred years it has been classed as a listed building, so has quite a few restrictions as to what you can and can't do to it. Grass grew everywhere and anywhere it could, roof tiles were missing and some of the brickwork needed repair.

It must be said compared to recent properties I've sold; this has to be one of the least appealing, yet exciting and challenging at the same time. I'll certainly have to work hard to do my magic on this one. Old twisted and fallen gravestones dotted down one side, only served to remind you what this place stood for in the community. Not believing in ghost or such like, one immediately got the feeling of calm and tranquillity, as the road ended at your front gate, before turning to a footpath leading you out to the surrounding countryside. The holly bush hedge interwoven with the rusty metal railings gave some indication as to how big the grounds are. Or would we call it a garden now? As I understand the area where the graves lie cannot be touched or altered in any way. Maintenance for that area would be carried out by the local diocese, who will have access via a separate entrance.

For someone who has the vision, I'm in no doubt this really could become a fantastic little home. And as for that large stained-glass window at the side, that's just to die for (sorry; couldn't help that!) With the right TLC just think what could be done? Dinner parties would need no planning regarding evening topics. Ongoing history you could call it, a new lease of life, the turning of a new chapter.

Delving into the past, marriages, christenings and of course funerals have all happened right here! Celebrations relating to Christmas and Easter to name but a few have all happened here. Wow!

Jumping right up to date, well only a few years ago civil partnerships were being recorded between same-sex couples. Congregations change with age; however, people must be prepared to accept change whilst still holding onto a sense of traditional morals and values.

I have to say it must be very confusing at times, being human.

Oh, to be a piece of wood.

## *Acknowledgements*

To my wonderful partner, Sue
and to my very dear daughter, Claire.

*Available worldwide online
and all good bookstores*

---

www.mtp.agency

www.facebook.com/mtp.agency

@mtp_agency

www.ingramcontent.com/pod-product-compliance
Lightning Source LLC
LaVergne TN
LVHW040202080526
838202LV00042B/3277